# HOW TO MAKE A POWERPOINT PRESENTATION

Best tips to create the awesome
presentation really fast!

Vicky D. N.

# HOW TO MAKE A POWERPOINT PRESENTATION

Best tips to create the awesome
presentation really fast!

Text Copyright © Vicky D. N.

Legal and Disclaimer

The information contained in this book and its contents is not designed to replace or take the place of any form of medical or professional advice; and is not meant to replace the need for independent medical, financial, legal or other professional advice or services, as may be required. The content and information in this book has been provided for educational and entertainment purposes only. The content and information contained in this book has been compiled from sources deemed reliable, and it is accurate to the best of the Author's knowledge, information and belief. However, the Author cannot guarantee its accuracy and validity and cannot be held liable for any errors and/or omissions. Further, changes are periodically made to this book as and when needed. Where appropriate and/or necessary, you must consult a professional (including but not limited to your doctor, attorney, financial advisor or such other professional advisor) before using any of the suggested remedies, techniques, or information in this book.

Upon using the contents and information contained in this book, you agree to hold harmless the Author from and against any damages, costs, and expenses, including any legal fees potentially resulting from the application of any of the information provided by this book. This disclaimer applies to any loss, damages or injury caused by the use and application, whether directly or indirectly, of any advice or information presented, whether for breach of contract, tort, negligence, personal injury, criminal intent, or under any other cause of action. You agree to accept all risks of using the information presented inside this book.

You agree that by continuing to read this book, where appropriate and/or necessary, you shall consult a professional (including but not limited to your doctor, attorney, or financial advisor or such other advisor as needed) before using any of the suggested remedies, techniques, or information in this book.

# CONTENTS

# INTRODUCTION

There will always come a time when a person has to make a presentation. Whatever the occasion may be, having visual cues that the audience can look at is much more effective than just talking. This helps increase understanding of the topic and makes them remember it easier.

Over the past few years, there is one program that dominates the slideshow presentation scene. This program is PowerPoint by Microsoft. This simple and easy to use program has been the go to software for anyone who wants to make a presentation.

This book will introduce Microsoft PowerPoint and its interface. It will also show you the basic steps on how to make a slideshow presentation. Tips and tricks to make your presentation stand out are also included.

# CHAPTER 1: POWER POINT

## The Basics

PowerPoint is a presentation program that lets you use slideshows to make visual cues for your audience. The slides are the most important part of this program. They are the main body of it and where most of the work is done. The slides are like cue cards that have the information in them. The types of information you can put in them is numerous. You can put in words or sentences. You can put pictures and charts. Graphs can also be placed. You can even play music or video files without having to change programs. PowerPoint has streamlined the presentation making process by integrating these key elements of the presentation into one program. Before we go on to the making of a presentation, let us first familiarize ourselves with the interface of Microsoft PowerPoint.

## The Interface of PowerPoint

## Presentation Gallery

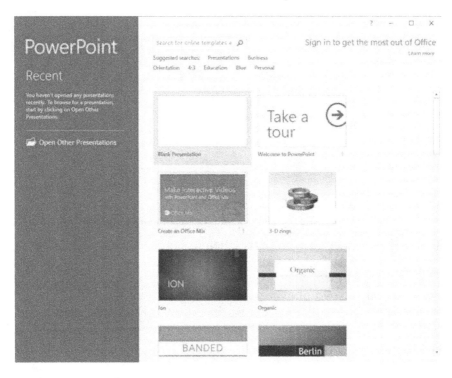

## The Presentation Gallery

The first thing you will see when you open PowerPoint is the Presentation Gallery. This Gallery shows some templates for certain presentations. The slides for these templates are already arranged and styled so that you won't have to. Each template also has a certain font that will help make your presentation look more beautiful or elegant. There is also a 'Blank Presentation' option. You may choose this if you cannot find a template that you like or one that fits your needs. This is basically making a presentation from scratch. The slides are not styled or customized so you will have to do this yourself. This is very useful when you are creating one for specific purpose or if you want your presentation to be as simple as possible.

## The Main Interface

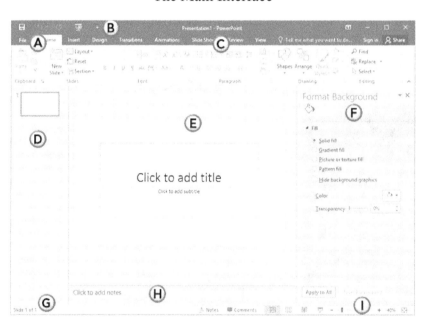

The Main Work Area with parts labeled.

This picture shows what you will see if you choose the 'Blank Presentation' shown above. This is the main interface of Microsoft PowerPoint. This is the main area that you work on. There are many parts of the main interface. These parts are the main tools that you use for creating presentations. Let's go through all the labeled parts of the Interface.

# File Menu and Backstage View (A)

## The Backstage View

The File Menu is where the controls for the document you are working on are. If you click on the File Button, you will be taken to the Backstage View. Here you can start a new document or open an existing one. This is also where you can find the Save button to save your work. The Print button allows you to print out the presentation.

## Quick Access Toolbar (B)

The Quick Access Toolbar, or QAT, is a bar that contains shortcuts to your most used actions. By default, it has the 'Save', 'Undo', Repeat, and Slideshow actions. There is a dropdown arrow which allows you to customize this bar to contain actions you may need.

## Ribbon (C)

The Ribbon contains the main options and editing tools you may need to create you presentation. These actions and options are arranged into tabbed groups making them easier to locate.

These Tabs include 'Home', 'Insert', 'Design', 'Transitions', 'Animation', 'Slide Show', 'Review', and 'View'. The Home Tab lets you control the fonts and their sizes. It is also where you can find the button to add a new slide to the presentation. The Insert Tab allows you to enter pictures, tables, graphs, and shapes to the slide. This is also where you go if you want to enter an audio or video file to the presentation. The Design Tab gives you the option to change the background of the slides. All the themes are shown and the variations of that theme. The Transitions and Animations tabs are very similar. They show the transitions and animations, respectively. There is also a button that lets you control the duration and when the animation or transition starts. The Slide Show tab lets you control the flow of the slideshow. There are buttons that allow you to start the slideshow from the first slide or from the current slide. You can also record the slideshow.

## Slides Pane (D)

The Slides Pane shows a 'zoomed out' view of all your slides. You can scroll to a certain slide without changing the slide you're working on. You may also rearrange the slides by dragging and dropping them.

## Slide Area (E)

The Slide Area is the main work area of PowerPoint. This shows the current slide you are working on. The options and actions you select on the Ribbon take effect on the current slide. You may also move and resize the text boxes on the slide.

## Task Pane (F)

The Task Pane automatically opens whenever a certain option is chosen in the Ribbon. Note that not all functions will open the Task Pane. The Task Pane contains more specific functions and that allow you to customize your slide. Most time the Task Pane is used to adjust pictures and to add effects to the text.

## Status Bar (G)

The Status Bar can be seen at the bottom left of the PowerPoint window and shows some basic information about the document.

It shows the total number of slides in the document and which slide you are currently working on. It may also show the language used by the program.

## Notes (H)

The Notes Pane is located directly below the current slide. Here you can put in notes about the slide. These notes will not be shown during the slideshow.

## View Controls (I)

Located at the right of the status bar, the View Controls change the way the slides are displayed. There is the **Normal View** which is the default view. The **Reading View** which allows you to look at all the slides much easier. The **Slide Sorter** shows clickable thumbnails of all the slides. The **Slideshow** plays a slideshow beginning from the current slide.

## Mini Toolbar

The Mini Toolbar

The Mini Toolbar is a small toolbar that appears when you click the right mouse button while text is highlighted. This floating toolbar allows you to quickly change some settings for the selected text.

## CHAPTER 2: HOW TO MAKE A PRESENTATION

Now that you've learned the basics of Microsoft PowerPoint, let's go and learn how to make a presentation from scratch.

Creating a Simple PowerPoint Presentation

Step 1: Open the PowerPoint App

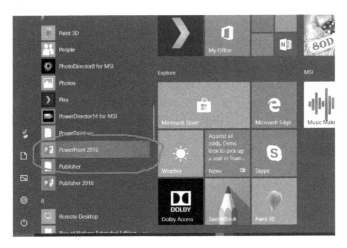

PowerPoint in the Start Menu.

Open the 'Start Menu' and look for PowerPoint 2016. Click on the icon to open the app.

Step 2: Check out the Templates and choose one that you like.

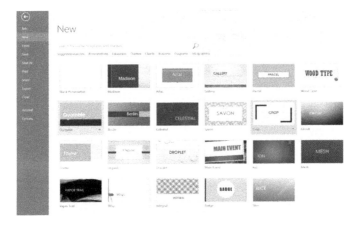

The Presentation Gallery

Upon opening the PowerPoint app, you will be taken to the opening page. Here you will see the available templates. The slides for these templates are already designed and have their own unique background and font styles.

Step 3: Choose available themes from the template that you chose.

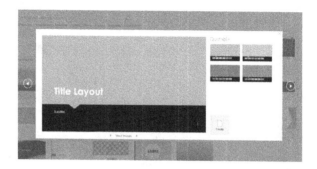

Choosing colors for the template.

Choose one that seems appropriate for the purpose of your presentation.

To select it, just click on the template you like. A dialog box showing the different variations of your chosen template will be shown. Just click the 'Create'' button once you have made your choice. But don't worry; you can change the style of your slides anytime.

Step 4: Create the Title Slide.

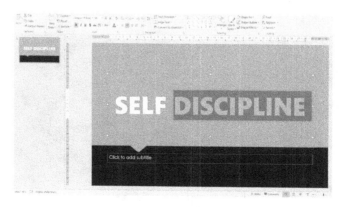

Putting in the Title of the Presentation.

Begin making the title slide of you presentation. Just type the title and adjust the font size and alignment. Try to keep the title short, maybe one or two words. There is also a subtitle section where you can add a more detailed description of the presentation. You may also move or resize the text boxes so that they will fit the plan you have for the slide. Next we will show you some ways to customize the text. Once you have chosen the font and its size, highlight the whole title to select it.

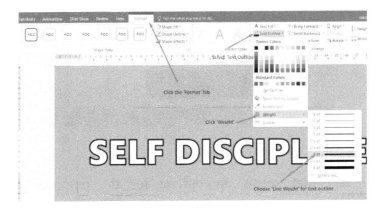

Customizing the text.

You can add some stroke lines to the text of the title to make it pop. Click the Format Tab on the Ribbon and click 'Text Outline'. On the dropdown menu, click the color for the text outline and its thickness.

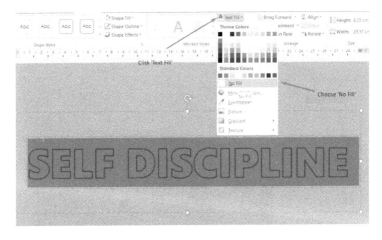

Changing the colors.

You can also change the color of the text. Just click 'Text Fill' and choose the color you want. In this case, 'No Fill' was chosen to leave only the outline of the text.

Step 5: Transitions

Setting up transitions.

Set up how the slide enters the presentation by using 'Transitions'. Click the Transitions Tab on the Ribbon and all the available transitions will be shown. Just click the arrows to reveal all of them. A preview of the selected transition will be shown when the mouse cursor is hovered on the icon.

Step 6: Create a new slide

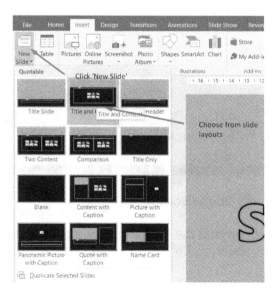

Adding a new slide.

To add slides to the presentation, click the 'Insert' Tab. Click the 'New Slide' button to show available layouts for the slide you want to add.

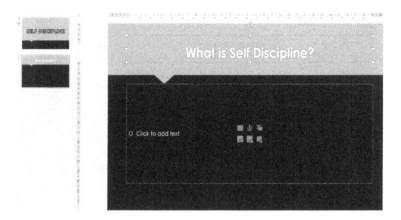

Adding in the text.

Once the layout of your new slide is selected, enter the text for it. Repeat this process each time you want to add a new slide. You may also choose different formats for tabs. You may choose ones that allow you to add pictures to it.

Step 7: Format Painter

The Presentation's title selected.

A quick way of copying the format or designs of text is through the use of 'Format Painter. To begin, highlight the text you want to copy.

Selecting Format Painter.

While it is highlighted, go to the 'Home' Tab and click on the 'Format Painter' button.

Applying the format to the new text.

Go to the text you want the style to apply on and highlight it. The style will take effect immediately.

Step 8: Adding pictures

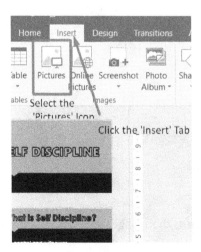

The Insert Tab and the Pictures button.

One good way of keeping your slides, and by extension the whole presentation, interesting is by using pictures. Pictures can be added easily in PowerPoint. On the 'Insert' Tab, click on the 'Pictures' icon.

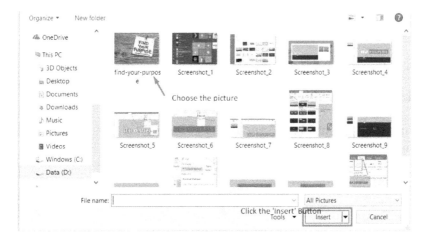

Choosing the image.

A new window will be opened where you can select the picture you want to add. Once you have chosen the image you want to add, click the 'Insert' button to add it to PowerPoint.

Resizing and adjusting the image.

Resize the picture in the slide. You can do this by clicking on the picture then dragging the circles at the edges and corners of the box.

Step 9: Customize your other slides.

A) Set up transitions

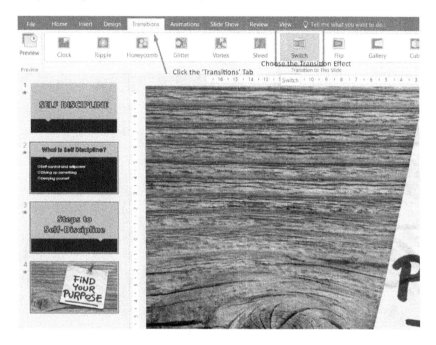

Setting transitions for multiple slides.

Select the slides and set up a transition for them. Click on the Transitions Tab and choose from the available transitions. A preview of the transition will show once you choose it. Try to keep the transitions simple and uniform. This will help keep the attention of the audience on the content rather than the effects.

Rearranging the slides.

You may also rearrange the slides of your presentation. Do this by dragging the thumbnail of the slide on the Slides Pane. Move it up or down depending on where you want it to be.

B) Animations

One way of controlling the flow of your presentation is through the use of animations. This is done by giving the text movement and only shows what you want to show.

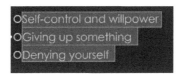

The text is selected.

Begin by highlighting the text you want to animate.

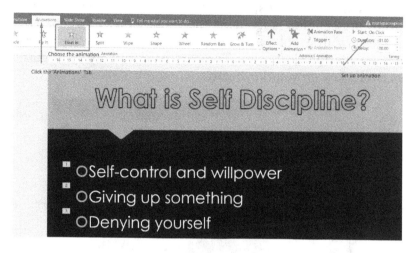

The Animations Tab and the available animations.

While the text is selected, go to the Animations Tab. Select the animation from the available options. To have full control over when the text will appear on the presentation, choose 'On Click' on the Start menu. Highlight each layer or group of text you want this to apply on. The numbers shown on the items is the order in which they will appear. Items with the same number will appear at the same time.

Step 10: Test Your Presentation

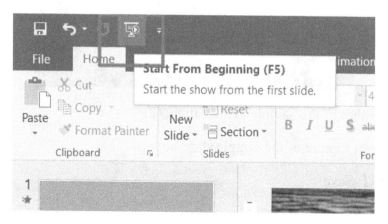

The Slideshow button.

After you have finished creating your slides and adjusting the transitions and animations, it is now time to test it. The best way to test your presentation is by using the 'Slideshow' function. To start the slideshow from the beginning, you may click on the Slideshow button on the Quick Access Toolbar. Alternatively, you can also press the F5 key on your keyboard.

Screenshot of the Sample Presentation. (1)

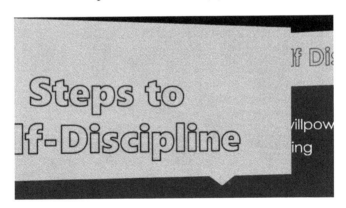

Screenshot of the Sample Presentation. (2)

A screen capture of the sample slideshow is.

Step 11: Save

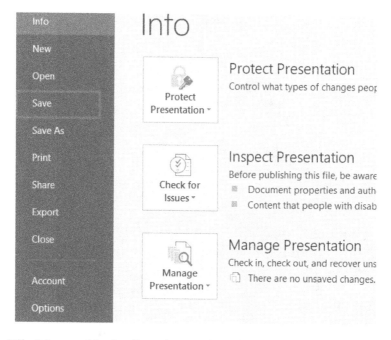

The File Menu with the Save button highlighted.

The final step in creating a PowerPoint presentation is to save it.

First, click on the File tab to open the Backstage View. Click on Save. Alternatively you may press 'Ctrl + S' on your keyboard to be taken directly to the Save menu.

The Save Menu.

This will open up the save menu. On the Save menu, click on Browse if you want to save it on a specific folder.

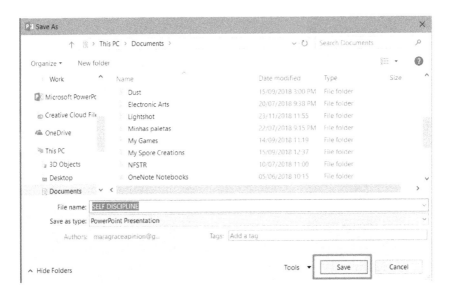

Saving the file to the folder.

A window will be opened and you can navigate the explorer to open the folder you want to save the file into. Once you have accessed that folder, put in a name for the file. A file name may be automatically generated by PowerPoint based on the Title of your work. After that, click the 'Save' button to save your presentation.

## Additional Options

The steps that we have given you this far are the most important in order for you to make a working PowerPoint Presentation. But there are more advanced options and settings in order to make your presentation look even better. We'll discuss two of the most common things that you may want to add to it.

## Adding Music

Sometimes, it may be necessary to add music or audio to your presentation. This is also a good way to make your presentation stick to your audience's memories a bit better. First, you will need to choose the slide where you want the audio to start. For this instance we have chosen to start the music on the first slide.

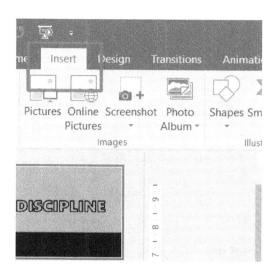

The Insert Tab.

Click on the Insert Tab on the Ribbon to open the Insert Menu.

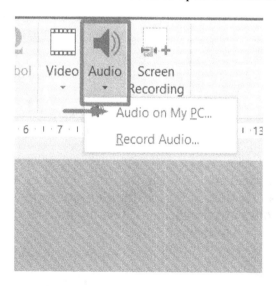

The Audio Button.

Click on the 'Audio' button to be able to add audio files to the presentation. Click on the 'Audio on My PC' to choose the file you want to add. You may also choose to record a new sound file.

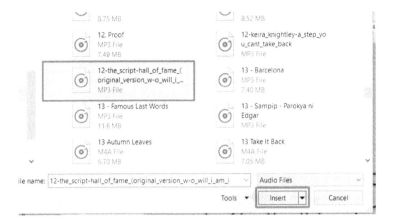

Choosing the audio file.

If you chose to add an existing file on your PC, a file explorer window will be opened. Navigate to the folder of the file you want to add and select it. To add it to the presentation, click on the 'Insert' button.

An error message.

An error message may pop up showing this message. What this means is that the format of the file you are trying to add is not compatible with PowerPoint. WAV files are the best file types to use when adding audio to PowerPoint.

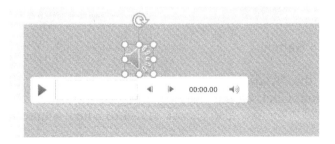

The icon for the audio file.

Once the appropriate file has been chosen, it will then be added to the presentation. A speaker icon will appear. You may test the file you added by clicking the 'Play' button.

Adjusting when and how the file will play.

After the file has been added and tested, configure it in order to customize the playback of the audio. Click on the 'Playback' button to open the playback menu. You may choose to have it play automatically when the slide starts. You may also have it play 'on click'. To make the music or audio play throughout the presentation, click on the 'Play Across Slides'. There you go, that is how simple it is to add audio and music files to your slideshow presentation. Adding music or audio will definitely make you presentation that much more interesting and memorable.

Adding Video

Another thing you may do to add more entertainment to your presentation is to add a video file. This is far more convenient than the other way of adding a video to your presentation. In this 'other' process means opening a video file and using a separate video player to play the file. Having a video play directly on PowerPoint it means that you don't have to switch between programs to play a video.

Selecting the slide.

Choose a slide where you want to add the video. This time we chose a new slide to add the video into.

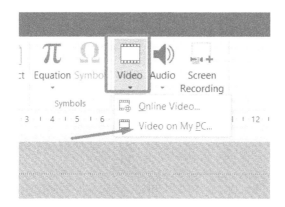

The Video button.

The process is similar to adding an audio file. On the Insert Tab, click on the 'Video' button. Click 'Video on My PC'.

Choosing the video file.

Choosing this option will open an explorer window. Go to the folder of the file and select it. Click the 'Insert' button to add it to the slideshow.

Testing the video.

Test the video to make sure that it plays correctly.

Resizing the video.

You may resize the video to make it fit the slide. Just click on the video window and drag the corner nodes. You may also move the video to a different location.

## Adding Tables

Tables are a necessary part of any presentation. They are used to show data in chunks that the audience can easily digest and understand. It serves two purposes at once. One purpose is that it presents the data for your audience to see. They can scrutinize it and see if what you're talking about makes sense. Another purpose is that it grabs their attention. It breaks the monotony brought about by the series of text and pictures in your slideshow.

There are at least a couple of ways to add tables to your presentation. You can add one manually and enter the data you need for each cell. Another is by linking tables from other Microsoft Office programs and integrating them to PowerPoint. We'll be showing you both of these methods.

## Manual Tables

Adding tables to PowerPoint manually is by going to the 'Insert' Tab and clicking 'Table'.

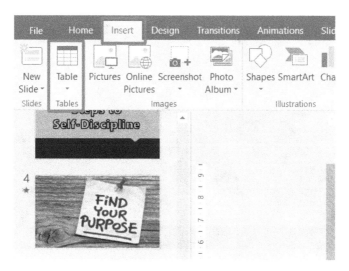

The Insert Tab and the Table menu.

This will open a dropdown menu with a series of boxes. These boxes signify the number of rows and columns that you may use for the table.

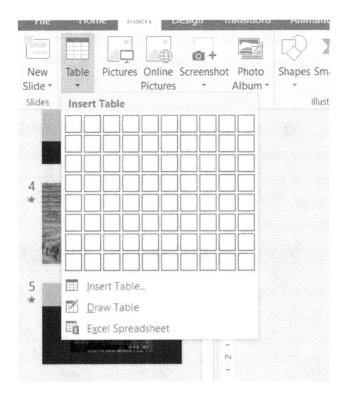

The grid for selecting the size of the table.

Once you have highlighted the number of rows and columns for the table, the table will automatically be added to the slide you are working on.

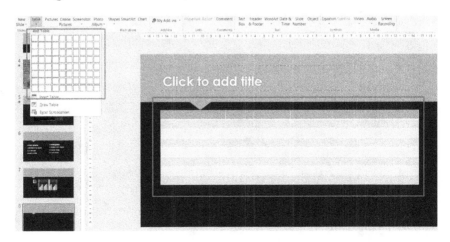

The table matching the size on the grid.

Once the table size is set, you may enter the data and the headings for the table manually. Take note that you will have to enter the value for each cell manually.

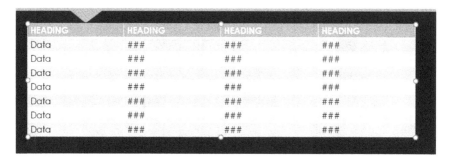

The data inserted manually.

## Table from Excel

Another way to add a table is to import one from Microsoft Excel. This option allows you to link the two programs to work together.

To begin, go to the 'Insert' Tab in PowerPoint. Next, click on 'Object'.

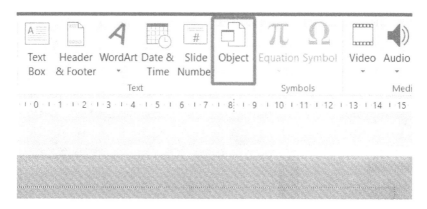

The Object button in the Insert Tab.

This will open a window that will allow you to open the file or file type that you want to add to PowerPoint.

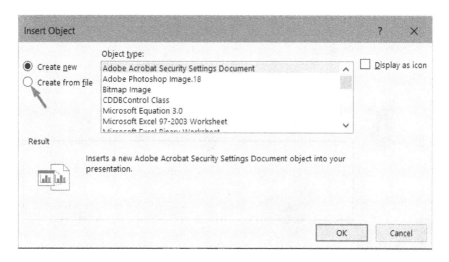

The Insert Object window.

To insert data from an existing file, click the 'Create from file' option. Click on 'Browse' to find the folder and file that you want to insert.

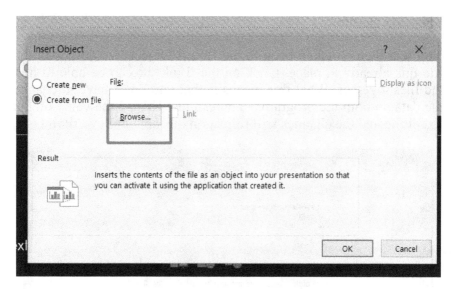

The 'Create from file' options with the Browse button highlighted.

After you found the file, select it and click Open.

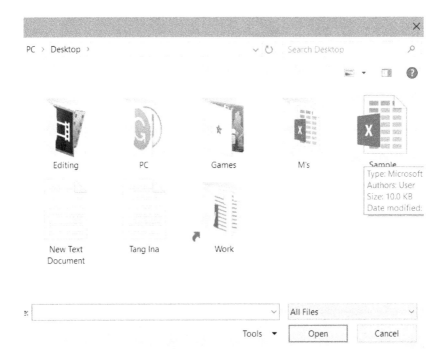

Choosing the file.

You will then be taken back to the 'Insert Object' window with the file link already in place. Click on the 'Link' box to be able to link the files together. What this means is that you don't have to change the data on both the programs. You can just change the value on the Excel file and the changes will reflect on the table in PowerPoint.

Clicking the link box.

| HEADING | HEADING2 | HEADING3 | HEADING4 |
|---------|---------:|---------:|---------:|
| Data1 | 2755 | 2813 | 3125 |
| Data2 | 58 | 312 | 719 |
| Data3 | 254 | 407 | 1146 |
| Data4 | 153 | 739 | 16486 |
| Data5 | 586 | 15747 | 49875 |
| Data6 | 15161 | 34128 | 88274 |
| Total | 18967 | 54146 | 159625 |

The data from the Excel file.

# CHAPTER 3: POWERPOINT TIPS AND TRICKS

In the previous chapter, we outlined the simple ways to create a PowerPoint presentation from scratch. The steps in adding music and video to your presentation have also been discussed. Now, we will be discussing things that will make your presentation pop. These are some tips and tricks to improve your presentation and make the most out of it. There is somewhat of a rule of thumb when creating a PowerPoint presentation. This rule says that the presentation should not be your whole speech. The slides are just something to catch the attention of your audience. Instead of having the slides become the focus, the audience's attention should be on you. In this section, we will outline some tips and tricks to follow this rule. We will be breaking these tips and tricks down to two categories: Preparation and Slide Design.

## Preparation

The most important part of any great presentation or speech is how you prepare for it. No matter how great you topic is, if you do not prepare for it properly, there is a big chance that no one will remember it. So, we will be discussing some ways to aid in preparing your presentation and, by extension, your speech.

## Research

Once a certain topic for your presentation, you will need to perform proper research for it. This is essential in order for you to have all the knowledge and information required for the speech. You will need to read up on a lot of things about the topic. Anything that you think can help your audience understand and, more importantly, remember the speech you are giving. Performing proper research entails reading a lot about the topic you want to talk about and you should learn more about it.

Any facts, figures, or data that you encounter may be of use to you once you begin your speech. This makes writing and planning your presentation easier. This also makes the whole process proceed much faster. Once you have read up on the topic, you will have to collate the information about it. Sort out the ideas and facts about it into categories. These categories will serve as the backbone for your piece.

# Planning

The next phase to creating the slideshow for your speech is to plan it. You need to plan how the speech flows and create the slides according to it. The slides should be pertinent to the part of your speech. The slides should show data, text or, picture that is relevant to what you are talking about. Another thing you have to think about is the general layout of the slides. How do you want your slides to look like? How many slides are needed for the whole speech?

Creating the outline of your presentation is the key to the planning process. One you have a solid outline, writing the speech and creating the slides for them will be much easier. The outline may also show unnecessary things in your speech. If there are any, remove them and replace them with some other ideas if needed. Having the outline as the basis for your slides also makes your job of creating the presentation easier. You will just have to use the topics and the subtopics as the content of your slide.

# Writing

This is probably the most important part of creating a presentation. In order for you to determine the flow of the speech and presentation, you will have to write your piece well. The advantage of having a great written piece is that the flow of the speech and the transitions between topics will be smooth. This will also aid you in creating your slides. Once you have finished writing your speech, test it out by reading it aloud. Are there any ways to improve it? Are there sentences that don't sound right? Edit these out and make sure that the speech you are going to give is smooth and flows properly between each topic.

# Slide Design

The 'bread and butter' of any good presentation are the slides in it. The slides are visual cues for the audience that helps them better understand the topic you are talking about. Any topic under the sun can be talked about. By extension, a presentation can also be created for any topic. In this section we will be talking about some tips that will make your slideshow a whole lot better.

# Simplicity

The number one rule when creating a slide is to keep it simple. How simple? As simple as possible. This makes sure that the audience keeps their attention on the content of your slide and not on the flashy stuff. Yes, having a different effect for every line on your slide can be beautiful to look at, but it takes away from your speech. If you create a 'flashy' presentation and you ask your audience what they remember after, most of them will probably say they remembered the effects and animations. If the purpose of your speech is to showcase all the effects and animations, then that is fine. But if it is not, having a lot of effects and animations will not only distract them from your speech, but it will also make them remember less about what you are talking about. Keeping things simple does not mean having a plain presentation. What you can do is to make the transitions between the slides uniform for the whole presentation. Having a single transition format makes the slides easier to follow. The animations for the contents of the slides should also be simple. Do not make the animations too flashy. Also, do not have a different animation for each bullet point. There are many animations available in PowerPoint, so try to choose ones that are simple and do not distract from your speech.

# PowerPoint 'Rule'

There no standard or yardstick against which we can measure every single PowerPoint presentation. Each presentation is unique and has to be. But there are certain 'rules' that people have discovered that make a PowerPoint Presentation more appealing. It also makes the speech easier to remember and follow.

# 2/3/6 Rule

There is a rule that is having some rounds. This rule is called the 2/4/8 rule. This rule is pretty simple. It governs the content of the slides and how the presentation as a whole flows. The rules are:

✓ Maximum of 1 slide every 2 minutes
✓ Maximum of 3 bullets per slide
✓ Maximum of 6 words per bullet

Now, let us explain how these rules work.

Having only one slide every two minutes gives you enough time to talk about the content of that slide. Of course you can spend more than two minutes talking about a slide, but you should allocate at least two minutes for each slide.

The maximum of three bullets rule makes sure that the text sizes will be enough so that even the people at the back can see them clearly. So if you have three bullets make sure that the size of the text is large enough so that you whole audience can read them clearly. There are of course some topics that cannot be broken down into just three bullets or less. What you can do with these topics is to break them up. Have just three bullets on the first slide and the rest of the bullet points on the next.

The human attention span is very short. This is especially more evident when we are reading. It takes a longer time for us to comprehend what we are reading when the text is long. So in order to have maximum retention and understandability for your slides, keep the content of each bullet point short. Six words or less has been found to be the most optimal length. This means that you don't have to put in whole sentences for each bullet point. This not only makes the text easier to digest and understand, but it also makes the slide look more pleasing. Having a lot of text on a slide makes it look more cluttered.

The audience's sightlines will stray from the topic. What's worse is that they will no longer listen to what you are saying. Instead they will just be reading what is in front of them. So try to put in just the topic or subtopic for each bullet point. Any definitions, if there are any, will have to be done by you. This ensures that their attention is with your speech and not the slides.

Presentations that are powerful and will make sure that you captivate your audience. There are other rules available out there that you may use. You may even modify this rule and experiment with it. The important thing is that you create a presentation that you are comfortable with and that conveys the proper message to the audience. Whatever the message may be, whether it is a school project or a business proposal, following these simple rules will make sure that you have a presentable and professional looking presentation.

## Text and Images

Most PowerPoint presentations contain either text or images. These words and pictures help convey the speaker's message to the audience. But a lot of people tend to just cram as much text into a slide as possible. This, as we have stated earlier, makes the speaker seem unprepared and not credible. So let us look into other ways to make your presentation look professional and make sure that the audience understands what you are talking about.

## Text Usage

The most important part of your presentation is the content. If you cram the whole text of your speech into the slides, then why are you still speaking? If all the text is in the slides, it will be better if you just show the slides and let your audience read the content. But that is not the purpose of a PowerPoint presentation. The slideshow should aid with your speech. It should not be the speech. What you are talking about is much more important than what is on the slides. The slides are there just to help the audience understand the topic much easier. So what are the ways that you can make the text in your PowerPoint presentation useful? Well, if you followed the rules stated earlier, you will have an idea of what needs to be done. First, keep the text short. The text in your presentation should be short and simple. It should be direct and to the point. Do not put any explanation on the slide. Do not put definition of terms in them as well. As was stated before, keep the content of each bullet to a maximum of eight words. What do we mean by not putting explanations and definitions on the slide? As is most often the case, especially among students, the definition of a term is often put in the slide. This is, to put it bluntly, a very lazy way to make a PowerPoint presentation. Your job as the speaker is to explain what is on the slides.

So what you can do is to just put topics or keywords on the bullets and slides. If there are terms and definitions on your slide, explain them verbally. Not only will this help you explain and define the term better, it will also help your audience understand the topic easier. What this essentially is you are breaking down the topic into chunks that are easier to understand. Second, use large font sizes. The most successful slideshow presentations are the ones that are easy to understand.

So how will the audience understand the content of your slide if they cannot see it? While you are creating your slides, use larger fonts that can be read from across the room. This works extremely well in conjunction with keeping the text short. If you use larger fonts, you will be forced to keep the text short. There may be some slides where a single word on the slide is enough to show the topic. What you can do then is to discuss this topic and explain it. Students are usually the ones who fall into the trap of putting as much information on the slide as possible. But they are not the only ones who do so. There are some professionals and working people who do not know of this. While it is understandable that they do not have enough time to learn everything, if presenting a slideshow is part of their job, they should be good at it. There are still some professionals who put in as much information in a slide. This is not solely because they did not prepare for it, but because they may have never learned the more pleasant way of making presentations. Some people mistakenly assume that because they can read it in their computer screens, the audience will be able to read it. But there is a simple workaround with this issue. What you can do is to look at the presentation from a few steps back. Play the presentation as a slideshow and take a few steps back from the screen. Five to ten steps should be enough. If you can still read the text in the slide without having to squint your eyes, then you're good to go. This simple test makes you look at the presentation form another angle — that of the audience. If you are able to see what they are looking at, you will be able to adjust your presentation accordingly.

Lastly, find the right font. This may seem a bit out of track but this is a common mistake that many people make. Most people, especially students, tend to use fonts that are fancy and have a lot of curves and extra lines. This makes the eye work harder than it has to, because it has to deal with all the other things in the text. This also affects fonts that are relatively simple. The fonts we mean are those with serifs. Serifs are the extra strokes that some fonts have. Fonts like these tend to make things harder to read. This is most evident if the colors are not black and white. Serifs are often used for things that are plain text and rarely, if ever, have any pictures. So what fonts are best used for PowerPoint? The fonts that are best used are those that are not fancy and don't have serifs. This makes the text easy to read and don't use up that much brain power. This reduces the amount of time the audience has to put in to the slide and the text therein, which means that they will have more time to listen to you.

The effects of serif and sans serif fonts.

This image shows the difference between the serif and sans serif fonts. The texts all have the same font size and they are all in uppercase letters. Notice that the sans serif fonts on the left are easier to read compared to the serif fonts on the right. It is also worth noting that the sans serif fonts also appear to be larger than their serif counterparts even though they have the same font size.

## Images in PowerPoint

So far, we have only been discussing the text as the content of your presentation. But presentations rarely, if ever, contain only text. Most presentations use pictures and images to help with the presentation. There are even some slideshows that use only images. Images and pictures help the audience relate what you are talking about with them.

There are a lot of advantages of adding images to your presentation. One of these is the correlation between the image and the topic. Most people are visual learners. They often need something to spark their minds to have an interest in something. That is why most advertisements make use of catchy pictures and images in order for the product to sell better. The images also help with the retention of any information presented. If you just show plain text to a person, they will not bother to look at it and read it. This is mostly due to the short attention span of humans. So what you can do to solve this is to use pictures. The picture you use must be related to the topic at hand. If you are telling a story, a picture that shows a certain part of that story will make the audience remember it and understand it better.

Pictures are not just attention grabbers though. They can also be used to convey the whole message. People often associate a memory or a feeling with a picture. Try this: Look at a picture of the beach. What do you remember? What do you feel? Most likely you will remember the warmth of the sun on your skin, the sound of the waves crashing into the shore or even the smell of the air. You may end up feeling more relaxed. Or you may feel like you want to go to the beach in order to experience those things once more. All of these feelings and memories are from just looking at a picture of the beach. Now imagine that effect happening to your audience while you are giving a slideshow presentation. Putting pictures in your presentation will make your audience remember things and feelings when they look at that picture. They may have experienced or seen something similar. Another effect this may have is in the future. If they see a similar picture after your presentation, they will remember the presentation that you gave and the information you presented.

Images also divert the audience's attention back to you. If there is a lot of text on the screen, the tendency is that the audience will read the text first before they listen to you. This is not because of any reason but due to the conditioning the human mind has received because of education. Ever since we were children, written text has been given more importance over spoken words. Because of this, we often pay more attention to written words. This will have an effect in your presentation if it is full of text. So what can you do to divert the audience's attention back to you, the speaker? Put some pictures in your presentation. If the image you show does not have any text, the audience will divert their attention back to you and focus on what you are saying.

These are just some of the ways you can use text and images in PowerPoint. There are multiple ways to do so. The program itself has the template for slides that incorporate images and text. Your job has already been made easier by these templates. You just have to capture the right images and words, and put them in your presentation. If there are some texts in your presentation, make sure that they are readable for everyone in the room. Make them as large and as simple as possible. Condense the information into small chunks that the audience will be able to understand easily. Use images that correlate with the topic and that evoke the specific feelings and memories that you want it to.

## Colors

Colors are very important in creating anything that people are going to be looking at. Choosing the right colors will most probably make presentation a lot better. Choosing the wrong ones will become a hindrance to your presentation. We use the terms 'right' and 'wrong' subjectively of course. Since the slides are personal we cannot say that there is a right color that will bring you and your presentation success. What we mean by these terms is the interplay between the colors. You may be asking, 'How do colors affect my presentation anyway?' Well, as we all know, the slides are there for the audience to see. So they must not only be functional but they must also be pleasing to look at. The colors you choose must be appropriate for the occasion and the location of your presentation.

## Time

The PowerPoint presentation you are creating will be certainly used for a specific occasion or time. So first, before designing your slides or determining what the images you are going to use, make sure that you know what the appropriate theme will be. If you are going to present for a formal meeting, you do not want your slide and presentation to look like a child's drawing, unless of course that is the theme of the talk. Earlier, we said something about the 'right' and 'wrong' colors. This is where colors come to the picture. Choosing the right colors will not only be for the benefit of the audience, but they will also help with the overall theme of the occasion. For example, you are presenting a PowerPoint presentation at a wedding, what are the most appropriate colors to use for the occasion? First of all, the wedding may have a color scheme. So you may incorporate that color with your slides. Now, as yourself this question, 'what is the most common color associated with weddings?' That color is white. So you may design your slides with that in mind.

You must also keep in mind the literal time when you will be presenting. Will you be showing the presentation in the day or at night? The time of your presentation will be a factor in the overall design of your slides because of the amount of ambient light. Make sure that the slides you are going to design are correct for the time of your presentation. Later we'll discuss it in more detail.

## Location

Next, you must know where you are going to present. The location of your presentation is a factor that is very similar to the time of your presentation. It will affect the amount of ambient light in the room, or lack thereof. This is the reason why books are read when there is enough light. Even though it is possible to read or see the text when there is low light, it puts a lot of strain in the eyes. The reverse can also be a detriment. This effect is best shown if you suddenly turn on the television in a dark room. The effect is that the eyes are suddenly bombarded with a lot of light and that tends to blind you for just a little bit. So the colors of your slides must be tailored to the room you are presenting. So, for example, you are presenting in a room with low light, a dark background with light text will be best suited. The inverse is true for a room with a lot of ambient light. In a room with a lot of light dark text over a light background will make sure that the text on your presentation will be readable.

## Text and Background Color

There are colors that don't mix very well when one is the background and the other is the foreground. But then, there are also colors that work extremely well together. This is the main idea in color theory. Everyone is familiar with the color wheel and what it looks like. This wheel shows the colors that we see. Of course there are some colors that are not in there but this is the most basic tool used in color theory. The best slides use principles of color theory to add intensity to it. The colors may also be used to direct the attention of the audience.

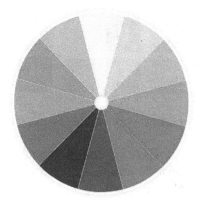

The Color Wheel.

Analogous colors are three, or more, colors that are adjacent to each other in the color wheel. The use of this concept will help you design backgrounds that are very pleasing to the eye. The colors that are analogous to each other work very well together. They create the impression of cohesion and unity. This picture is an example of the use of analogous colors.

An image that uses complementary colors.

Complementary colors are the opposite each other in the color wheel. Even though they are opposite each other that does not mean that they will not work well together. Complementary colors are often used to show or create emphasis. In relation to designing your slides, it is best to use the complement of your background color.

An image showing the good ways of using contrast.

This image shows the effects of complementary colors. Notice that al the letters are very visible and that they look crisp and sharp. This is also the effect that you want to achieve when designing your slides.

Another concept we have to look at is about contrast. Contrast is the play between the colors. This deals more with the 'darkness' or 'lightness' of the color. Let's look at the image below to see the effects.

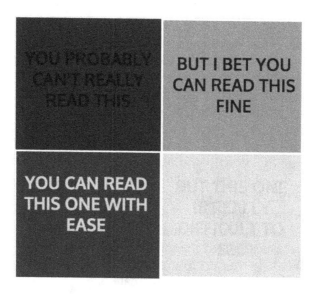

An image showing the effects of good and poor usage of contrast.

If you notice the top left and bottom right colors are a lot harder to read. Meanwhile, the other two can be read at a glance. This image shows the proper use of contrast when creating colored text. The text is there to be read so you have to make sure that it is easy for the audience to read. Using a dark text on a dark background will make this very hard because the dark text 'blends' with the background. Having light colored text on a light background will also have this effect. So it is best to use a mix of both light and dark.

If you have a light background, make sure that the text you are using is dark. This color scheme, light background and dark text, is best used for times where there is a lot of light. Meanwhile, if the background you chose is dark use text that is lighter that is a lot lighter than the background.

This is best used for times when there is low ambient light. Just to be safe for text colors, using black or white never goes wrong. And the good thing is, they work well with everything, provided that the contrast is right.

## Custom Themes

There may be times when the templates that PowerPoint provides does not suit the purpose you have. It may be because of the special theme of the talk you are going to give. It may be because you don't like the templates. Whatever the reason may be for going away from using the templates, there is a very simple solution to that. You can just create a custom theme for the presentation you are planning to create. Having a customized and personalized theme will help make your presentation fit the overall theme of the talk. If you were not the only one giving out a speech, it will make you appear to be in sync with the other speakers while still making your presentation unique. The look and visuals of your slides will also be more pleasing. And, more importantly, it will ultimately work for the benefit of your audience. It will work because they can relate the custom theme you create to the talk you are giving. Even if you are the only speaker, it is helpful to have a personalized and customized theme for your talk. It will help the audience remember what you talked about. But how do you make a customized theme? Will it be fiddly? Will it be hard to do so? What do you do to create one? Well, we have compiled some simple instructions on how to create one.

## Changing the Colors

First, let's start simple. Let's say there is a template from PowerPoint that you want to use. There is one issue: you don't like the colors in it. What can you do? Well, you can change the colors. First, you will need to go to the Design Tab and choose the theme, if you have not selected one yet.

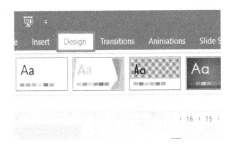

The Design Tab.

On the 'Variants' section, you will see a dropdown arrow. Click on it and all the variations of the theme will show up.

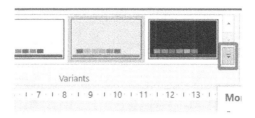

The button to show all designs.

There are also other items in that list, namely 'Colors'. Click on this to show all the available colors that you can use for the theme. Keep in mind that these color schemes are available for all PowerPoint themes. Mouse over the colors to see how they affect the slide.

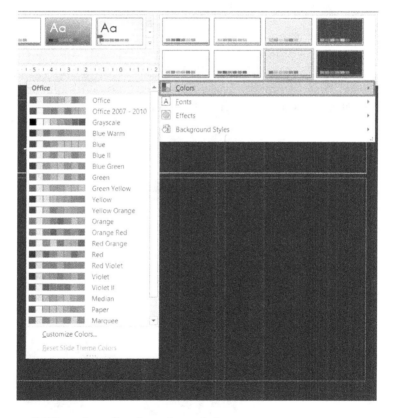

The available colors for the selected theme.

Don't worry if the colors that are on the options still do not appeal to you. There is still a way that lets you customize the colors even more. At the bottom of the menu, you can click 'Customize Colors'.

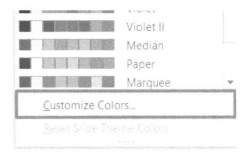

The Customize Colors button.

This option allows you to fully control the colors of the theme. You can change all the colors of the theme so that it will suit your needs. Once you are happy with the colors, click 'Save' to apply the color changes to your document. The changes in color will appear on the 'Sample' area so you can see how the colors play with each other.

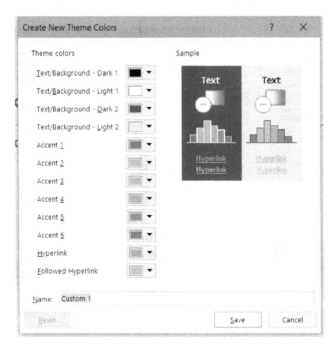

The window for customizing colors.

# Changing the Fonts

Next, we will be talking about the fonts that come with a certain theme. As we have talked about before, certain fonts are better suited for PowerPoint presentations than others. Fonts that do not have serifs will be better that those that have. This is because of the overall shape and readability of the typeface. In this section, we will be discussing how to change and customize the fonts that a certain theme will use. To change the fonts of a theme, you first have to go to the Design Tab and click the dropdown arrow on the Variants section, as shown previously. This time, though, click on the 'Fonts' option.

The Fonts button.

This will show a menu having all the fonts. You can scroll down the menu and mouse over them to see how they will change the slides. If you have chosen one, just click it and it will take effect on the document.

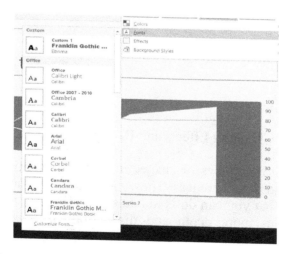

Available fonts for the document.

However, if you do not see a font that you want to use for the theme, you can still customize them. Click on the Customize Fonts button to open up a new window.

The Customize Fonts button.

This window will allow you to further customize the fonts on your theme. You will see the changes take effect on the Sample area. For this menu, all the themes you have in your computer will be shown. And here you can also set the theme for the body of the slide. If there is any text in the slide other than the heading, this is where you can change it so that it will be harmonious with the rest of the slide.

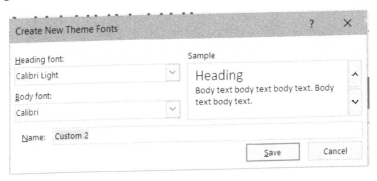

Customizing the fonts.

### Changing Effects and Background Styles

If there are any graphics or shapes in your presentation, they may appear flat and dimensionless. They appear as what they are, shapes with color. What you can do is to add some effects to these graphics and give them more depth and dimension. To customize these effects, go to the Variants section on the Design Tab.

On the dropdown menu choose Effects.

The Effects button.

Once you click on it, there available effects will show. Mouse over one of them to see how they change the graphics on your slide.

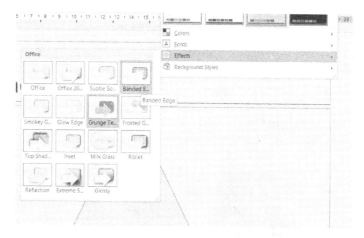

The available effects.

The Background of your slide is the biggest graphical piece in it. The background contains all the elements of the slide. It is basically the stage for all of you text, graphics, and images. PowerPoint lets you choose the color of your background. But you can go further than that. You can change the background and customize it further. To customize the background, go to the Variants section on the Design Tab. Click the dropdown arrow and click on 'Background Styles'.

The Background Style button.

This will show all the background styles available based on the theme colors you have chosen. The images will have different variations like gradients and shadings.

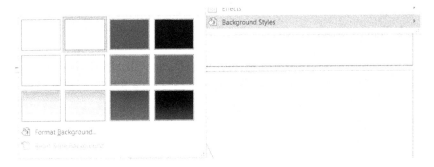

The available background templates.

If you want to customize the background further, click on the 'Format Background' button. This will open the Task Pane.

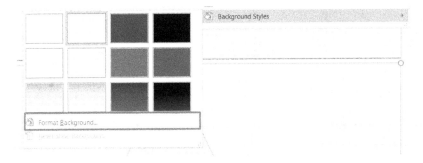

The Format Background Button.

On the Task Pane, which will be on the rightmost part of the PowerPoint window, you will see different options that will allow you to change the background. If you want the background to be a single color, click on Solid Fill. On 'Color' you can change the color of the background while the transparency bar lets you customize how opaque or transparent you want the background to be.

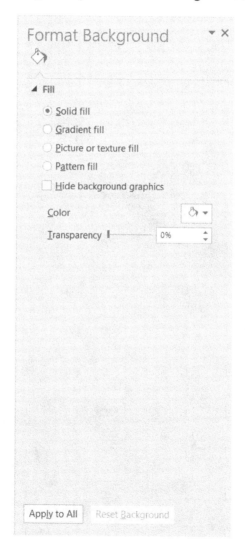

The Format Background Menu.

Gradient Fill lets you apply a gradient effect to the background. You can change the type, direction, and angle of the gradient. There are even some preset ones that you can use. The Gradient Stops let you change the position of the different colors of the gradient effect. Each stop may be set to a different color so you can create a two-tone gradient effect. You can put in as many colors as you can to create the background you want.

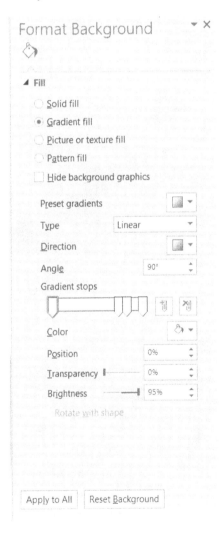

Adjusting the background's gradient effect.

Picture or texture fill lets you put a picture instead of colors as a background. This is helpful if you want an image to be the background instead of being in the slide. It is also great if you want a more detailed and intricate background that PowerPoint cannot offer. You can choose the file you want to use as the background from your folders by clicking the 'File' button. There are also some textures that you may use instead of a picture. If the 'Tile picture as texture' box is ticked, the picture you choose will be arrayed in order to create a tile effect as the background of the slide.

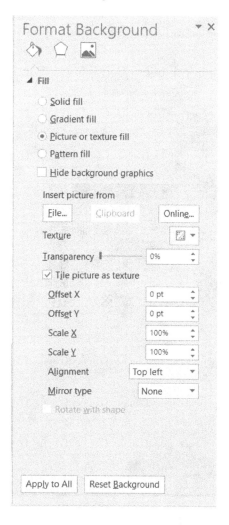

The Picture or Texture fills options.

Pattern Fill will give you a set of patterns to use as a background. These are simple two color backgrounds that will give texture to the slide. You can customize the colors of the pattern by changing the Foreground and Background colors. The changes in color will show up on the patterns in the task pane. You may mouse over each pattern to see how it will look like on the slide.

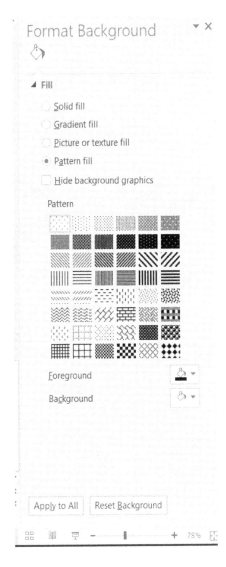

The Pattern Fill options.

Once you have chosen the background and customized it, you can apply the changes to the slides. You can create a different background for each slide of your presentation. Or you can click the 'Apply to All' button to have the background you designed take effect on all the slides in the presentation.

Trying It Out

We have discussed the basic and some advanced ways to create a PowerPoint presentation. What you now have to do is to do it on your own. The guidelines and rules we have outlined here are not made of stone. They are not solid, unbendable, and unbreakable rules. You can break some of them and mold them to suit your style and your needs. The rules are there to serve as guides in order for you to be able to create a good, professional-looking, and memorable PowerPoint presentation.

Now in order for you to see this in action let us use an example. You are going to present a report in school. You were tasked to use PowerPoint for this presentation. In order for you to create the best PowerPoint presentation possible answer these questions.

✓ How will you make sure that the audience understands the topic?
✓ How many slides are you going to use?
✓ What images are you putting in?
✓ What do you want the audience to feel while you are giving your presentation?
✓ What do you want them to remember about it?

Answering these five questions will make sure that the PowerPoint presentation you give is memorable. It will help your audience understand the subject you are talking about.

# CONCLUSION

Slideshow presentations have been around for a very long time. Ever since the advent of photography, people have been using slideshows to give speeches and provide information about certain topics. Now, in the $21^{st}$ century, the computer has taken over the world. Almost everything can be done and created using computers. Slideshow presentations were not exempted from this. Microsoft's PowerPoint program has changed the way people create slideshow presentations ever since it was launched. It has not only changed the way information is presented, it has also become a staple for those in business and school. PowerPoint's interface is easy to follow. The tools and options needed to create a presentation are all at hand. They are just a mouse click away. Editing and designing slides is also easier and faster because of the templates available for use. Creating a PowerPoint slide can be summed up in a few steps. First, pick a background and layout. Second, enter the text or image for the slide. Third, pick the transitions and animations for the slide and its contents, respectively. Adding other media like audio clips and videos has also been streamlined. With just a few mouse clicks, music or a video can be played without having to change programs. Creating an interactive PowerPoint presentation has never been easier. There are some things you need to do first before creating a PowerPoint presentation. You first have to research for the topic that you will be discussing. Doing so will help you plan the presentation, which is the second step. The plan or outline you have created based on your research will serve as the backbone of your speech and presentation. Having a well-written speech will make sure that the audience will remember the presentation. It will also make sure that they learn what you want them to. There are some rules regarding the design of the slides. The most important of these is to keep the slide simple. Remove any distractions from the topic. Avoid using 'flashy' animations and transitions. These tend to take away from the presentation. The 'rules' on how to design your slides are the 2/4/8 Rule and the 10/20/30 Rule. These 'rules' are guidelines on how to design a slideshow presentation that the audience will remember. PowerPoint uses a combination of text and images to relay the speaker's message. Proper use of these tools will ensure that the message will be received by the audience without any misunderstanding. The slide should not be cluttered with too much text. Use large texts that can be seen even those farther away.

Images are very useful for speakers. They make the audience relate with the topic. They also make them remember thoughts and feelings about the image. They are attention grabbers and redirectors. They help keep the audience's attention on you and your speech. There are many ways to make PowerPoint presentations. There is no single guidebook that tells you to 'do this' or 'do that'. Instead, they serve as guidelines for creating presentations. They can be bent and broken depending on the purpose of the presentation. Just remember a few things about a slideshow presentation. The slideshow should not be the main focus of your presentation. Instead, the focus must be on you and the topic you are talking about. The slideshow should not distract the audience from the topic. It is there to aid with the speech. It is not the whole speech. Keep this in mind and your slideshow presentation will definitely be remembered and appreciated by your audience.

Please leave a review on **AMAZON.COM**. Once you have read this book, why not leave a review on the site that you purchased it from? Potential readers can then see and use your unbiased opinion to make purchase decisions; I'll see your feedback and understand what you think about my book. Thank you!